the Noble
HORSE

the Noble
HORSE

Angela Rixon

southwater

This edition is published by Southwater

Distributed in the UK by
The Manning Partnership
251–253 London Road East
Batheaston
Bath BA1 7RL
UK
tel. (0044) 01225 852 727
fax (0044) 01225 852 852

Distributed in Australia by
Sandstone Publishing
Unit 1, 360 Norton Street
Leichhardt
New South Wales 2040
Australia
tel. (0061) 2 9560 7888
fax (0061) 2 9560 7488

Distributed in New Zealand by
Five Mile Press NZ
PO Box 33-1071
Takapuna
Auckland 9
New Zealand
tel. (0064) 9 4444 144
fax (0064) 9 4444 518

Southwater is an imprint of Anness Publishing Limited
© 1994, 1999, 2000 Anness Publishing Limited

1 3 5 7 9 10 8 6 4 2

Publisher: Joanna Lorenz
Project Editor: Clare Nicholson
Assistant Editor: Charles Moxham
Designer: Edward Kinsley
Jacket Design: Clare Reynolds

Previously published as *Horse*

The publishers would like to thank the following photographic libraries for their kind
permission to reproduce their photographs:

(Abbreviations: b = bottom, m = middle, t = top, r = right, l = left, i = inset)
Animal Photography/Sally Anne Thompson 9tl and 12. Bruce Coleman Limited front cover image.
Bruce Coleman Limited/Jane Burton 7 and 13t. Bruce Coleman Limited/Christer Fredriksson 25.
Bruce Coleman Limited/Michael P Price 11. Bruce Coleman Limited/Hans Reinhard 46/47. Bruce
Coleman/Johnathan T Wright 28. Kit Houghton 1, 9tr, 13b, 19b, 26b, 49, 53, 54/55, 58/59, 60t,
60b, 61t, 67t, 69, 70b, 71t, 71b, 73, 73i, 74, 79r, 86b, 89 and 92. Bob Langrish 2, 5, 6, 8t, 8b, 9b,
10, 14, 15, 17, 18, 19t, 20, 21t, 21b, 22, 23, 24, 26t, 27, 29, 31, 33b, 35b, 36, 43t, 43b, 44/45,
44i, 45, 50t, 50b, 51t, 51b, 56, 57, 61b, 62, 63t, 63b, 64, 65, 66, 67b, 68, 70tl, 70tr, 72, 76, 77,
78, 78i, 79l, 80, 81, 82/83, 84, 85, 86t, 87, 88, 89i, 90, 91, 93t, 93b, 94, 95 and 96. Solitaire
Photographic 30, 32t, 32b, 33t, 34t, 34b, 35t, 36b, 37, 38t, 38m, 38/39b, 39t, 40t, 40b, 41 and
42. Survival Anglia/Terry Andrew Artha 48 and 52.

Page one:	The enquiring stare of a grey discovered in a woodland glade.
Page two:	An Arab horse on a stud farm.
Page three:	Grass is the natural food of all horses and ponies.
Page five:	A laughing horse.

CONTENTS

HOW HORSES BEHAVE 7

BREEDS 31

HORSES AT WORK 49

COMPETITION 69

How Horses Behave

*A*LL THE behaviour patterns of today's many breeds and types of domestic horses and ponies can be directly linked to those displayed by their early ancestors in the wild. Horses slowly evolved from a terrier-sized creature with four long toes to the sturdy, single-hoofed animal we know today. More than two hundred and fifty intermediate species of fossil ancestors of today's horses have been discovered, identified and named, representing over fifty million years of evolution. The earliest horses lived furtive lives as browsers in deep forest regions; but, as they gradually evolved, horses adapted to grazing, and changed their habitats to open grass plains and prairies.

Opposite Most indigenous British pony breeds can withstand harsh weather.
Below A New Forest foal dozing.

The first equines to be domesticated by humans were onagers and asses (donkeys), close relatives of the horse. True horses were probably first harnessed by the Chinese about 5000 years ago, and used as willing and obedient pack animals. Over the succeeding centuries horses were selectively bred for tasks such as pulling chariots. Eventually human beings learned to ride.

Top Mares are always very vigilant while their foals suckle, however safe and secure their environment might seem.
Right A young Welsh foal enjoys the warm spring sunshine.

Above left Young male horses (colts) practise their fighting techniques in the paddock.
Below left Today's domesticated horses often run freely just for sheer enjoyment.
Above A Shetland Pony seeks grass beneath a deep covering of snow.

MARES AND THEIR FOALS

A YOUNG HORSE or pony is a foal; male foals are called colts and female foals fillies. They reach adulthood at four years of age, fillies becoming mares and colts becoming either stallions or, if they were castrated at an early age, geldings. While stallions are highly spirited and can be difficult to manage, either for riding or as work-horses, geldings are easily trained, good-natured and willing.

In the wild, mares start breeding at about two years of age and, if conditions are favourable, can produce a foal every spring after a gestation period of about 340 days. Mares produce very rich milk and suckle their foals for months, even after the youngsters have learned to graze efficiently for themselves.

Wild stallions fight for superiority and for the privilege of serving all the mares in the individual's own small herd. Young colts nearing maturity are driven from the main herd and often form small all-bachelor herds, away from the mares and fillies.

Opposite The sides of a pony mare nearing her term bulge with the burden of the foal inside her.
Below Assateague Island horses often suffer from lack of grazing. Here a thin mare feeds her foal while her daughter from the previous Spring stands close by.

Mares generally give birth to singleton foals; twins are rare, and sometimes fail to survive. The mare lies down for the final stages of the delivery, getting up again once the foal has been born. She instinctively licks her baby and nudges it to its feet. Most foals stand up shortly after birth and soon get their long, spindly legs under control. The mother continues to nuzzle and nudge the foal, encouraging it to find her udder. From the moment of birth the mare and foal are inseparable, and the mother will put herself between her foal and any potential source of danger. She may resent humans or other animals approaching or touching her foal, and will kick and bite in its defence. The foal itself has a set of inborn defensive actions: it is able to run alongside its mother soon after birth, and can buck and kick hard.

Above A foal naturally stays close to its mother's side at all times, a behaviour pattern inherited from its wild forebears.
Opposite above The foal's spindly legs are difficult to control at first, particularly when it is getting to its feet.
Right As it grows older and stronger, the foal practises defensive tactics such as rearing, bucking and kicking out.

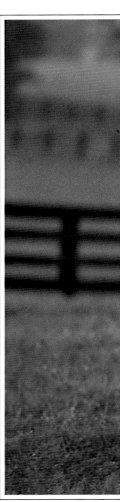

Foals are fascinating to watch, particularly if several mares and their offspring are kept together. Each foal has its own distinct personality, but innate behaviour patterns continue to come to the surface. All the instinctive characteristics of the horse's wild ancestors are exhibited in a foal's play behaviour. It nips at its mother and playmates, biting at their necks and lower legs. If there is any retaliation the foal will wheel around and playfully kick back in pretended anger. It will often jump high in the air and kick backwards at an imagined enemy, or leap sideways. With its head down and its back arched, it will buck furiously in circles around its mother.

Opposite A young foal nips playfully at its mother's head.
Above This one has learned to scratch behind its ear with a dexterous hoof.

HERDING

*T*HE HERD instinct is very strong in all members of the horse family, wild or domesticated. Horses are able to run together for long distances over rough, undulating ground without putting a foot wrong. The herd moves almost as a single entity, guided by senses that we humans are unable to comprehend.

In the wild state, the weakest members of the herd succumb to predators, leaving the strongest and fittest members to survive and breed further generations of successful and healthy individuals.

Right A herd of wild Mustang race across the Nevada prairie.

COMMUNICATION

ORSES AND ponies are able to express a whole range of emotions through their behaviour and body language. Their very mobile and dilatable nostrils can be expanded and contracted at will to register emotions such as interest, fear and bad temper. The ears, too, are mobile, and the movement of the nostrils is often connected with the direction in which the animal's ears are held. When the ears are pricked forward the horse is interested or alertly listening to some sound; if they are laid back the horse is displeased. The eyes of the horse are of course very expressive. Even the attitude of the tail can be used to read a horse's state of mind.

Horses use their full range of expressions when meeting and greeting each other, and often recognize the body signals faster than we can. Horses use sounds to emphasize their body signals, ranging from a soft, gentle whickering to a shrill, angry squeal. Stallions are able to scream and roar, and mares have a special whinny reserved for their foals. Many horses neigh to greet their owners.

Opposite above On meeting, horses blow into each other's nostrils. The chestnut has its ears pricked with interest; the brown horse presents a warning signal, with its ears laid back.
Opposite below A mare is delegated to guard duty while her companions take an afternoon nap.
Below Greetings between old friends in the stableyard.

GRAZING

*D*OMESTIC horses seem at their happiest when they are turned out, with companions, into large areas with plenty of good grass. Horses graze by swinging their heads from side to side as they move forward, biting off mouthfuls of grass close to the roots. The grass is passed to the back of the mouth to be thoroughly chewed at the same time as more grass is being harvested.

Opposite Grazing on a perfect green pasture.
Left A healthy Percheron eats meadow grasses contentedly.
Below As well as grazing in lush grass, horses love to roll in it whenever possible.

MOVING AROUND

*M*OST HORSES and ponies used for riding have four distinct natural gaits. The slowest is the **walk**, which is performed in four-time – that is, the horse takes four separate steps one after another in a set sequence. Faster than the walk is the **trot**, a lively gait in two-time, in which diagonally opposite hindfeet and forefeet are moved in synchrony. In the **canter** the horse moves in three-time, and you can clearly hear the three beats to each full stride. At the end of the cantering stride the horse momentarily has all four feet off the ground. This graceful gait can be performed by the horse on either the right or left diagonal.

Above This Arabian mare clearly demonstrates the brief moment in each cantering stride when all four feet are simultaneously off the ground.

When a horse canters on the left diagonal, the sequence of steps is as follows: off-side (right) hindfoot; nearside (left) hindfoot together with offside forefoot; and, finally, nearside forefoot. When it canters on the right diagonal, the sequence is the reverse of this. The canter is a comfortable gait for the rider and not too strenuous for the horse.

The **gallop** is the horse's fastest gait. It is in four-time – that is, it is not merely a very fast canter. The legs move individually in the sequence near-hind, off-hind, near-fore, off-fore again; at the end of this sequence, as in the canter, the horse is suspended for a moment above the ground. This is the gait you can see in racehorses as they strive for the finishing post.

Below A group of Arabian horses just beginning to stretch out into a full gallop.

YOU, THE HERD LEADER

*T*HE ANCESTRAL wild horse was a gregarious animal, accustomed to living as a member of the herd and to obeying the general directions of the herd leader. Even today, the horse retains this need for companions and a leader; it is this latter requirement that has enabled it as a species to be so readily tamed and trained. Once a horse has been isolated from its fellows, it will look to its handler for direction. If a trainer takes a young horse out on its own into a quiet paddock, he or she can control it on a long lunge rein, allowing the animal to move in its natural way and in natural gaits, praising acceptable behaviour and correcting whatever might be undesirable. Gradually, the horse learns to follow the directions given by its "new leader", and more sophisticated lessons can be taught in a similar fashion. Most early training is carried out in this way, with the trainer on foot and the horse on a long rein.

Opposite A fine stallion rearing. This is a natural behaviour which must be curbed by careful training.
Below Even in captivity, stallions will fight for supremacy.

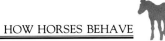

A COMFORTABLE LIFE

THE DOMESTIC horse enjoys an organized life. It is content to carry out work from time to time seeming to give the matter very little thought so long as it has a comfortable environment with food and water whenever it wants them.

The horse has a very keen sense of smell. This helps it find the tastiest food: it can locate tender shoots buried beneath snow or submerged in shallow water. Water itself is another consideration. Allowed a free choice, horses drink only from fresh, untainted sources, such as clear streams. In the stable, they should be given water before each feed, and there should always be plenty of clean, fresh water available.

Opposite left The typical grey horses of the Camargue region of France graze on succulent shoots submerged under water.
Left Most horses are quite fearless of water, and will happily gallop along the seashore at low tide or even take a swim.
Above Horses and ponies enjoy drinking from natural streams.

ANCESTRAL MEMORIES

*T*HE INFLUENCE of the past on the horse of today is visible in almost everything it does. The horse is a natural prey animal, not a predator, and so all its reflexes and instincts are directed towards self-preservation. The slow side-to-side movement of the head as the horse grazes is an example: the eyes are set in the head in such a way that the horse can see all around itself while grazing – even directly behind, by looking between its legs.

Some defensive behaviour can be irritating. Even a docile horse may shy at a strange object or totally refuse to enter a gateway. Such behaviour has been coded into the horse over millions of years. Offset against these nuisances are the many advantages the horse's behaviour patterns have given us, notably the willingness to accept human beings in the place of equine herd leaders.

Below The wild Mustang in Nevada have not exchanged freedom for the food and comfort of a life of domesticity.
Opposite Even domestic horses are perfectly capable of foraging for their food in winter conditions.

Breeds

Y CONTROLLING matings between domestic horses, humans were able to interfere with the natural selection process in order to develop horses gradually for specific purposes. Over the generations, desirable characteristics were strengthened and unwanted traits bred out, until some countries – and even regions within countries – had their own, easily distinguished horse and pony breeds.

Opposite The Shetland Pony is a tiny breed which has existed in the Shetland and Orkney Islands, to the north of Scotland, for 2000 years.
Below The Norwegian Fjord, a primitive pony type, has the erect mane and colouring of the Wild Horse.

Far left The natural colour of the wild desert horses is still seen in some of today's breeds.
Far left, below The Percheron is a breed descended from early warhorses.
Left A naturally thick coat and full mane keep the Shetland Pony warm in all weathers.
Below A group of Przewalski or Mongolian Wild Horses.

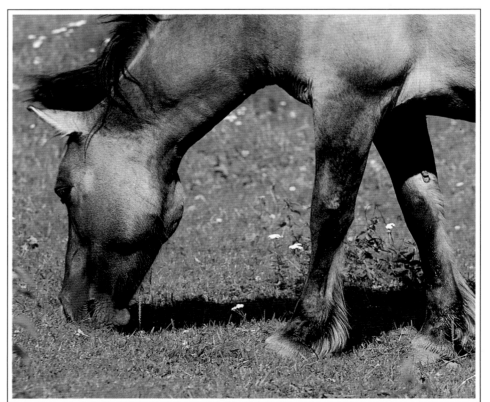

ANCIENT BREEDS

*T*ODAY'S OLDEST form of horse is the Przewalski or Mongolian Wild Horse. Survivors of this breed were discovered in the Gobi Desert in 1881, and it has been conserved in zoos and parks worldwide. Another breed, the Tarpan, did in fact become extinct, but careful back-breeding programmes have reconstructed it in its living form in Poland, and herds have been reintroduced to the wild.

Opposite above The Wild Horse is golden dun in colour with a naturally erect, dark mane.
Opposite below The reconstructed Tarpan living free in Poland's forests.
Above The magnificent Shire Horse is descended from warhorses.
Below The Dutch Heavy Draught, massively built and very strong.

The horse's natural colouring was originally dun – golden dun for desert-dwellers and a darker mouse-dun for forest-dwelling horses like the Tarpan. Other colours were gradually brought to the fore through cross-breeding and mutation.

Right The Norwegian Fjord Pony's distinctive erect mane.
Below In addition to the basic dun, this pony has a dark dorsal stripe and black legs, just like the Przewalski Horse.
Opposite The Haflinger breed from Austria has a bright chestnut-coloured coat.

Above Dartmoor ponies were originally used for pack-work, over very rough ground, or as pit ponies.
Right The Exmoor Pony is thought to be the descendant of the British Wild Horse.
Below Lundy Island, off Britain's west coast, has its own pony breed developed from Exmoor and Connemara ponies.
Opposite Of the four Welsh breeds of pony, the Welsh Mountain Pony is smallest and lightest.

BREEDS

NATIVE PONIES

D URING THE last Ice Age, wild horses were often forced into discrete pockets of land, and so today many countries have their own distinctive breeds of small horses, known as ponies. The British Isles are renowned for their selection of diverse pony breeds.

From Scotland come both the largest and the smallest of the British ponies. The tiny Shetland Pony is immensely strong for its size, and very hardy. In the past it often had to exist on the seaweeds and lichens of the islands and work hard for its living as a crofter's pack-pony. The Highland Pony is descended from an old race of horses that existed before the last great Ice Age. There are two types: the large Garron, which was used in agriculture and forestry, and a smaller type, which makes a perfect riding pony.

Opposite Native ponies are products of their environment.
Opposite below Though small, the Shetland Pony is strong. It was once used to haul heavy carts in coal-mines.
Below Highland Ponies are naturally hardy, and can withstand even the coldest winters of their native Scotland.

COLOURS

*J*UST AS horses and ponies with the physique required to perform certain tasks were selected for breeding, so certain colours and coat patterns were regarded as interesting. When an attractive or unusual coat appeared, attempts were made to preserve it in future generations. The result was that certain characteristics became genetically fixed in isolated communities, such as in remote regions or on islands. Today, for example, the Lipizzaner of Austria, the Camargais of France and the Kladruber of Czechoslovakia are always grey, while the Frederiksborg of Denmark, the Haflinger of Austria and Britain's Suffolk Punch are always chestnut.

Above Palomino is a colour-type rather than a breed. Palomino horses and ponies have golden coats and flaxen manes and tails.
Right top Appaloosa horses, with their spotted coats, were first bred by the Nez Percé Indians of North America.
Right below A handsome and boldly marked Spotted Pony.

THE THOROUGHBRED

*A*NOTHER TRAIT important in the horse's development was speed. The Thorough-bred can trace its ancestry to three Arabian stallions imported to England about 300 years ago. These were mated with selected mares, and further selective breeding produced the swift, sleek cup-winners of today. Thoroughbreds have been used to refine other breeds, enabling some countries to produce their own racehorse varieties.

Below The influence of Thoroughbred bloodlines can be seen in the elegant lines of this mare's refined head.
Main picture A herd of Tersky horses in the Caucasus Mountains, bred up by introducing Arabian bloodlines.
Opposite The influence of Thoroughbred or Arabian bloodlines can be seen in numerous breeds around the world.
Following page The Arabian, the oldest and perhaps the most beautiful of all today's domesticated horse breeds.

Horses at Work

OR CENTURIES horses were used as pack animals, carrying goods of all kinds between great cities. Then came the development of the horse-drawn coach to transport people and their belongings along main routes; by the seventeenth century the stage coach was in vogue. Ploughing and heavy agriculture were originally undertaken using teams of oxen, but by the end of the eighteenth century, with the development of heavy breeds, horses had taken over most of the work of the plodding oxen.

Opposite Heavy horses harnessed to a farm wagon laden with bundles of corn to be taken back to the farmyard.
Below Built for speed rather than pulling power, a working horse of Morocco.

Today there are far fewer working horses than in the past, although those still in use are expected to give a full day's work for their keep. Horses are used by the police and army, in agriculture, in sport and for entertainment – for example, in the circus ring and at the rodeo. With the depletion of the Earth's energy resources, working horses may come into their own again in the future.

Opposite above Mexican riders use their horses in the ring in a roping demonstration.
Opposite below A Hungarian horseman rounds up a herd of Furioso horses.
Right A proud rider astride his lightly built Tunisian pony.
Below A group of working ponies herding cattle in Nevada.

SHIRE HORSES

ODAY'S HEAVY-HORSE breeds are descended from the great warhorses of long ago. As firearms were developed and armour discarded, lighter mounts were needed for battle, and so heavy horses were instead deployed on the farm. Most countries of the world have their own breeds of heavy horses, many of which still work as they have for centuries. Heavy horses have found other roles, too: pulling brewery drays for advertising purposes, competing in the show ring and appearing in parades.

Opposite Cutting hay with a pair of sturdy Shire Horses.
Below An immaculate pair of brewer's horses trot into the ring.

ON DUTY

*A*LL OVER the world police horses are used to help control traffic and crowds. The horses need to be carefully selected and stringently trained if they are to perform their tasks effectively and without giving way to fear. In most police units each horse has one particular rider assigned to it.

Like the police, the army expects its horses to put in a good day's work. They encounter many of the same problems in basic training as do their counterparts in the police, and in addition have to perform in parades, often working in close formation with other horses.

Previous page A perfectly matched team of Suffolk Punch Horses ploughing. This breed is always chestnut in colour.
Opposite Mounties – members of the Royal Canadian Mounted Police – take their matched horses on parade.
Below Members of the Cadre Noir cavalry school of France presenting a traditional display of High School riding.

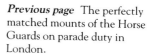

Previous page The perfectly matched mounts of the Horse Guards on parade duty in London.
Far left An immaculate turn-out of both horse and rider.
Left Members of the Beaufort Hunt set off for the day.
Below left A Huntsman with his pack of English Foxhounds.
Below Riding sidesaddle cross-country is a great skill.

Opposite A Lipizzaner stallion.

Top This great drum horse is always under control.

Left Lipizzaners of the Spanish Riding School of Vienna perform faultless displays of High School movements.

IN THE CIRCUS

*A*LTHOUGH ANIMAL acts in circuses are generally frowned upon, it does seem that horses enjoy performing in the ring almost as much as audiences enjoy watching them. Acrobats or clowns may balance precariously on the back of a cantering horse, individual horses may perform feats of obedience or skill, or teams may work as Liberty horses, carrying out routines closely resembling those of the great cavalry schools, often in time to selected music. The training given to circus horses is exacting, for they must be able to work in a very confined space, under artificial lights and with lots of distractions.

Below A troupe of Liberty horses start their wheel routine. The muzzles are to prevent them nipping one another in excitement.
Opposite A fine pair of Arabians performing in the circus ring for their accomplished acrobatic rider.

THE RODEO

T HE RODEO is a development from impromptu exhibitions put on by cowboys to demonstrate their skills in working with animals. At the rodeo riders compete in such events as calf-roping and bull-riding, using tough, highly trained horses.

Opposite An Australian bronco tries its best to dislodge a top rodeo rider in the ring.
Left A cutting contest, in which a horse and rider cut out a cow from the herd.
Below A display given in traditional costume.

Competition

FOR CENTURIES people have used horses in all manner of sporting pursuits. The trend has continued into modern times, and today people from all walks of life take the opportunity to indulge in equine activities. As well as horse-racing, popular pastimes include show-jumping, eventing, hunting, polo, gymkhana, trekking and hacking.

In the racing world, horses may be used "on the flat", where speed and sometimes stamina are tested, and for steeplechasing, where jumping skills are required as well. Especially in North America, there are race meetings also for trotting horses, in which the jockeys ride lightweight carts called sulkies at high speed around the track.

Opposite The Swedish rider Peder Fredricsson competes on Hilly Trip at the 1992 Olympics.
Below Michael Roberts on Monix.

Far left, top A Thoroughbred in a fast flat race at Santa Anita.
Opposite top Kyra Kyrklund on Vancouver II in the testing dressage section of the Goodwood Three-Day Event in 1993.
Opposite below A fine Hackney performs at the British Driving Show, Windsor.
Above John Whitaker on Henderson Hilton in fine style at the Hickstead International Ground, 1990.
Left Jayne Harrison on Crackdown copes well with the gruelling cross-country section at Loughanmore, 1992.

Below Emile Faurie on Virtu.
Opposite The epitome of elegance. Nicole Uphoff on Rembrandt performs the dressage test at the 1992 Olympics.
Opposite inset Klaus Balkenhol on Goldstein exhibits the desired control of movement required in international dressage.

EVENTING

*T*ELEVISION coverage of equine sports has increased public awareness of the very special skills such competitions require of both horse and rider. Quite different sets of abilities are tested in the three separate disciplines involved in any Event, whether it be over one day or three; these disciplines are dressage, cross-country and show-jumping. The same horse and rider must compete in all three parts to show that together they have mastered the quite distinct forms of training required.

The Three-Day Event was introduced to the Olympics in 1912, and today is an extremely popular component of the Games.

Left Staffan Lidbeck on Bernhardino. The cross-country section of an international event includes all manner of strange obstacles.

The dressage tests which form the first section of an Event are designed to show what degree of obedience the horse has achieved. The set movements consist of basic schooling exercises involving changes of pace and direction. The strenuous endurance section of an Event is completed over a steeplechase course and cross-country; it totals 17 miles (27.4 km) and is exhausting for both horse and rider. The third and final phase of an Event is performed back in the ring: show-jumping tests controlled jumping ability.

Opposite Ian Stark on Murphy Himself racing through water during the cross-country phase at the 1992 Olympic Games. *Above* In the same Event, Eiki Miyazaki, riding Mystery Cargo, likewise finds that the water jumps cause few problems.

SHOW JUMPING

SHOW-JUMPING HAS always been popular, and has attracted an enormous new following through coverage on television. It can be held in either an outdoor or an indoor arena; interestingly, some horses display a marked preference for one or the other. In most competitions the scoring system does not depend on the simple accumulation of points; instead, contestants receive penalties (known as "faults") for knocking down fences or refusing jumps. The various styles of jump test the horses' ability to clear considerable heights, to jump breadth as well as height, to clear stretches of water and to change direction, often at high speed. A fence is considered to be knocked down if any part of it is dislodged. If a horse refuses to jump a fence three times, it is disqualified from the competition. The time taken for the round often enters the calculations as well.

Opposite The famous show-jumper Henderson Milton, ridden by John Whitaker, performs with classic ease, tucking up his legs to avoid dislodging the high poles.
Opposite inset Robert Smith on Silver Dust at the dreaded bank of the Hickstead International Jumping Course.
Below left and right Otto Beckel on Lucky Luke and Anne Kursinski on Cannonball clearing posts and rails, designed to test skill and accuracy in high jumping.

DRIVING

A LTHOUGH DRIVING horse-drawn vehicles for transport has been practised for centuries, the art of driving emerged as a fashionable pastime only towards the end of the eighteenth century. Today the sport of driving is gradually gaining in popularity. Combined driving, officially recognized as a sport from 1969, is the equivalent of Three-day Eventing, but on wheels. Competitors are assessed on presentations, complete a dressage test and then compete in a cross-country marathon over a course about 18 miles (29 km) long, during which six hazardous sections must be negotiated. The final phase, back in the arena, consists of accurate driving through markers.

Above HRH Prince Philip is an accomplished driver and enjoys combined-driving tests. Here he turns his perfectly matched team of Fell Ponies at the top of a steep ascent.

Another popular contest, obstacle driving, is usually held in an indoor arena. In this fast and extremely exciting event, teams of ponies hurtle around a twisting course negotiating up to twenty obstacles in a battle against the clock. Obstacles knocked over attract time faults.

Show driving takes place in the ring, with the emphasis being on the smartness of the complete turn-out, including the horses, the vehicle and the driver, who is referred to as the "whip". Competitors enter the ring and circle one behind the other, being told by the judges when to change direction. The judges note the action of the horses as the teams trot around the arena, and call the teams in to line up one by one. They then assess general presentation and ask each driver to give a short solo performance, finishing with a neat halt and a straight rein-back.

Below A typically testing hazard in a cross-country marathon: taking the team along a stretch of river bed.

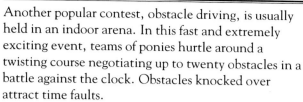

FLAT RACING

*T*HE MOST popular single equestrian sport is racing. The first records of horses being raced date back to Ancient Greece in about 600BC. Both the Egyptians and the Romans were fond of competitive and dangerous sports, and they staged mounted races as well as chariot races. Today few countries do not have their own horse-racing fraternity, with bands of ardent punters attending meetings and betting on the results. There are also countless armchair punters, who follow the races on television or radio or in the newspapers.

Previous page A four-in-hand team of greys speeds down into a river-bed hazard at the bottom.
Below Early morning is the time to see Thoroughbred horses in training, working out on the gallops (galloping tracks).
Opposite An impressive string of Thoroughbred horses walking to the gallops to go through the daily training routines.

85

STEEPLECHASING

STEEPLECHASING and point-to-point racing developed from hunting, when riders made private wagers as to the prowess of their mounts at speed over hazardous terrain. The most famous steeplechase race in the world is the Grand National, held at Aintree in England; it was first run in 1839.

Right This grey horse is the world-famous steeplechaser Desert Orchid.
Opposite A worm's-eye view of the field clearing a jump.
Below The Sun Alliance Steeplechase at Cheltenham. Steeplechasers must jump at speed and have the stamina for long distances.

The Thoroughbred horse of today is a living racing-machine, but most of the many Thoroughbreds born each year are not destined to run on the track: only the fastest and most talented are likely to pay their way in this expensive and highly competitive sport. The majority of Thoroughbred colts are gelded and, along with fillies, are usually sold as riding horses for hacking, hunting and performance in the show-ring.

Promising yearlings go to one of the specialist sales rings, and if of good breeding and conformation may be purchased and put into a training yard. Experienced trainers bring out the best in the young horses, and the cream of the crop will try for top honours in the Classic races. At the end of their racing career successful horses are retired to stud, with the mares annually bearing a new foal sired by a stallion with an impressive record.

Above In the USA much flat racing takes place on a dirt or sand track rather than on grass.
Opposite The best of the year's horses race to the finish of the Kentucky Derby.
Opposite inset Nostrils flaring with effort, three Thoroughbreds strive for the finishing post at Gulfstream, Florida.

RETIRING TO STUD

A FAMOUS STALLION will, on retirement, command an impressive stud fee for servicing approved mares. Specialist stud-farms house one or more stallions, each of which is allowed to service about 40 mares per season. Mares come into season shortly after the birth of a foal. Stud-farms therefore accept mares while they are pregnant, attend to the birth of the foal, and then supervise matings with the designated stallion.

Below The versatility of the Thoroughbred is displayed in St Moritz, where the track is formed of impacted snow.

TROTTING

URING THE 1960s, interest in harness racing – usually called trotting – began to increase in many parts of the world. Trotting has always been a major sport in the USA, and some horses have achieved international reputations for their speed. The equivalent of the Thoroughbred is the standardbred, and standardbreds can have pedigrees every bit as impressive as their Thoroughbred cousins.

Harness races fall into two categories, trotting and pacing, depending on the gait in which the horse runs, although "trotting" is used generically for both types of race. After a short run-up to the start, competitors race around a circuit, with the main rule being that the specified gait – trotting or pacing – must not be broken. There is also a handicap system, whereby horses that have proved very fast in previous races have to start behind their slower rivals.

Above Harness racing is an exciting sport in which, either trotting or pacing, horses draw lightweight sulkies at breakneck speed around the track.

POLO

*P*OLO ORIGINATED in Persia some 2000 years ago and was adopted as a sporting game by British cavalry officers in the nineteenth century. Polo players must be superb riders, and must spend hours of practice in order to perfect the art of hitting the ball while their mount is travelling at full gallop. Polo is, with the exception of ice hockey, the fastest game in the world. Polo "ponies" are over 15 hands in height, and are thus usually in fact horses. They must be fast, obedient and capable of very sudden starts and stops. There are four players in each team, and a game consists of four to six periods of play (chukkas), each lasting seven and a half minutes, with a three-minute rest period between chukkas.

Opposite above Polo ponies are trained to work fast in close proximity to one another, and to be totally responsive to the riders' aids.
Opposite below Not all polo matches are played on grass. Here in St Moritz surefooted ponies and riders battle on snow.
Below Despite the rider's shift of weight, the experienced polo pony continues to race in a straight line for goal.

STARTING YOUNG

*C*OMPETING IN Pony Club meetings and gymkhanas improves the riding techniques of young people. Such activities also help improve the ability of the ponies, which seem to enjoy them. Most of today's top competitive riders will affirm that their interest started with such events.

Right Children learn to school and ride their ponies more efficiently if they take part in organized mounted games.
Below A very competent young rider, with an excellent seat and good hands.
Following page Even young children can become confident enough to ride at speed over quite solid obstacles.